D1327489

# Ss

Kelly Doudna

Published by SandCastle™, an imprint of ABDO Publishing Company, 4940 Viking Drive, Edina, Minnesota 55435.

Printed in the United States.

Cover and interior photo credits: Artville, Comstock, Digital Stock, Eyewire, PhotoDisc, Stockbyte

Library of Congress Cataloging-in-Publication Data

Doudna, Kelly, 1963-
    Ss / Kelly Doudna.
      p. cm. -- (The alphabet)
    ISBN 1-57765-439-0 (hardcover)
    ISBN 1-59197-019-9 (paperback)
    1. Readers (Primary) [1. Alphabet] I. Title.

PE1119 .D6863 2000
428.1--dc21

00-056901

The SandCastle concept, content, and reading method have been reviewed and approved by a national advisory board including literacy specialists, librarians, elementary school teachers, early childhood education professionals, and parents.

## Let Us Know

After reading the book, SandCastle would like you to tell us your stories about reading. What is your favorite page? Was there something hard that you needed help with? Share the ups and downs of learning to read. We want to hear from you! To get posted on the ABDO Publishing Company Web site, send us email at:

**sandcastle@abdopub.com**

# About SandCastle™

A professional team of educators, reading specialists, and content developers created the SandCastle™ series to support young readers as they develop reading skills and strategies and increase their general knowledge. The SandCastle™ series has four levels that correspond to early literacy development in young children. The levels are provided to help teachers and parents select the appropriate books for young readers.

**Emerging Readers**
(no flags)

**Beginning Readers**
(1 flag)

**Transitional Readers**
(2 flags)

**Fluent Readers**
(3 flags)

These levels are meant only as a guide. All levels are subject to change.

**ABDO**
Publishing Company

To see a complete list of SandCastle™ books and other nonfiction titles from ABDO Publishing Company, visit **www.abdopub.com** or contact us at:
4940 Viking Drive, Edina, Minnesota 55435 • 1-800-800-1312 • fax: 1-952-831-1632

Sally has fun with Sara.

Sandy holds her sister.

Sancho slips on sunglasses.

Sam sits on the sidewalk.

Selma sits in a swing.

Sen eats supper.

Sue slides in the sand.

Susan sits in the sun.

# What is Sid doing?

(swinging)

# Words I Can Read

## Nouns

A noun is a person, place, or thing

fun (FUHN) p. 5
sand (SAND) p. 17
sidewalk (SIDE-wawk) p. 11
sister (SISS-tur) p. 7
sun (SUHN) p. 19
sunglasses (SUHN-glass-iz) p. 9
supper (SUHP-ur) p. 15
swing (SWING) p. 13

## Proper Nouns

A proper noun is the name
of a person, place, or thing

Sally (SAL-ee) p. 5
Sam (SAM) p. 11
Sancho (SON-choh) p. 9
Sandy (SAND-ee) p. 7
Sara (SAIR-uh) p. 5

# Verbs

A verb is an action or being word

# More **Ss** Words

saddle

sailboat

soccer ball

stop sign

24